D1716928

A PLAY

Words by
Claire Boiko and Therese Angress

Pictures by
Tony Tallarico

A GOLDEN GATE JUNIOR BOOK
CHILDRENS PRESS, CHICAGO

**Library of Congress Cataloging in Publication Data**

Boiko, Claire.
  My hero!

  "A Golden Gate junior book."
  SUMMARY: The Pauper family is in a quandry; they
have no money for the rent and Mean Mac McMiser means
to collect.
  [1. Plays] I. Angress, Therese, joint author.
II. Tallarico, Anthony. III. Title.
PN6120.A5B64438        812'.5'4        78-11505
ISBN 0-516-08887-4

# Characters

Mean Mac McMiser          Lovely Lily Pauper
    Handsome Harry Hero          Papa Pauper
        Narrator

**Narrator** Ladies and gentlemen, your attention, please. The Popcorn Players are about to present the drama of the ages—or at least the week! Prepare to laugh. Prepare to weep. Prepare to gasp—as you witness thrills, chills, and the meanest man in fifty states. Ushers will pass among you with smelling salts and kleenex, in case you are overcome! And now, the curtain rises on the humble home of humble

6 old Papa Pauper, a man who hasn't had a day's work since 1913. His daughter, poor but proud Lily Pauper, just lost her job selling matches on street corners. The family is down to its last mouldy soda cracker. The snow is snowing, the wind is blowing, the rent is due, and Papa is in bed with the flu, pneumonia, measles and a bad case of hangnails! Listen!

**Papa Pauper** Lovely Lily, my poor but proud daughter, the rent is due today. What shall we do? Listen to that wind. Oh, I'm sick as a dog!

**8**     **Lovely Lily**   Do not worry, Papa Pauper, my dear old white-haired father, all will be well. I will appeal to the landlord, Mean Mac McMiser. Only a beast would put a poor family out in the streets on a day like this. *(There is a knock at the door.)* Pray enter, whoever you may be.

**Papa Pauper**  Oh, 'tis you, Mean Mac McMiser.

**McMiser**  Yes, 'tis me, Papa Pauper. Your rent is due. In fact—it's overdue. You haven't paid a cent of rent since 1913. Now, pay up—or—

**McMiser**   Get out. Out, out into the snow and the ice and the bitter, bitter cold. However, if you can't pay the rent, I have another proposition. I'll take a little "something else."

**Lovely Lily**   Something else? But we have nothing                    11
to give you.

**McMiser**   Oh, yes you have, Lovely Lily, poor but
proud beauty. *You.*

**Lovely Lily** Me!

**Papa Pauper**   Well, he doesn't mean *me*, Lily. Oh,
no, dastardly McMiser. You would not take an old
man's only comfort—next to his hot water bottle?

**Lovely Lily**  No, no, a thousand times no! Not if you offer me silks and satins. Not if you offer me diamonds. Not if you offer me a steak dinner. Well—maybe if you offer me a steak dinner. No!

**McMiser**   A McMiser never takes no for an answer.   15
You will come away with me, if I have to drag you
by *brrrute force.*

**16**    **Papa Pauper**    Help, help!

**Lovely Lily**    Help me! Oh heavens, someone! Come to my assistance. I am being abducted by *brrrute force!*

**McMiser**    Heheheheh. I have you in me power now, proud beauty. You are mine. Mine, do you hear?

**Lovely Lily**   Oh, save me! Save me! It's your last chance, someone! Going—going—
*(Enter Handsome Harry)*

**Handsome Harry**   Unhand that female!

**Lovely Lily**   Handsome Harry Hero! At last! What took you so long? I expected you on the first "help!"

**Papa Pauper**   Get him, Harry. Get McMiser.

**Handsome Harry** So—foul fiend, McMiser. We meet again. Take that, you rascal. And that, and that!

20    **McMiser**   Oh! Oh! Ooh! Please—not the profile. Don't mess my profile!

22  **Papa Pauper**  He's up. Now he's down. There's a right to the jaw, and a left to the shoulder!

**McMiser**   Stop! Halt! Enough! No more hitting. In addition to being a McMiser on my mother's side. I'm a McCoward on my father's side. I surrender.

**24** **Handsome Harry** Had enough, eh? Go back to your rat hole, you wretch. Or, go back to your wretch hole, you rat. Be gone. Scat. Shoo. In other words, get lost.

**McMiser**   Yes, sir. Right away, sir. I'm begoning. I'm
scatting. I'm shooing. In other words, I'm getting lost.

**26** **Lovely Lily** Handsome Harry! My hero! How can I ever repay you? I would ask you to stay for supper, but we have but one mouldy cracker to share.

**Handsome Harry**   Never mind, poor but proud Lily.   27
I need no other food but the food of love. Let me feast
my eyes on you. Besides, Lily my sweet. I own a
delicatessen.

28 **Lovely Lily** A delicatessen! Oh, Harry, I'm in heaven!

**Papa Pauper**   What about me, Harry? I'm still sick as a dog.

**Handsome Harry**   Courage, Papa Pauper. I can cure
you.

**32**   **Handsome Harry**   In addition to being a delicatessen owner, I'm a *veterinarian!*

**THE END**